RVING ON THE
WRONG SIDE OF THE ROAD

A HANDY GUIDE FOR SCREWING UP

I. MICHAEL GROSSMAN

PUBLISHER'S INFORMATION

EBookBakery Books

Author contact: imichaelgrossman@verizon.net

ISBN: 978-1-953080-53-0

DEDICATION

To any RV camper who's busted pipes after winterizing, whose overfilled tires, whose backed into a tree you could swear was never there or whose been stranded by the side of the road waiting for the tow truck company that swore several hours ago, they'd be there any minute.

And to Susan and Lauren

ACKNOWLEDGMENTS

Thanks to the many YouTube video channels that provide useful information - even if it wasn't enough to keep me from 101 blunders. Among my favorite channels (and there are others):

Chris Dunphy & Cherie Ve Ard - *Mobile Internet Resource Center*
Jason Epperson's - *RV Miles*
Chad and Tara Florian (and Daisy) - *Changing Lanes*
Jared Gillis - *All About RVs*
Tod Henson - *Tech Tip Tuesday (National RV Training Academy)*
Marc, Tricia (and Charlie) Leach - *Keep Your Daydream* (KYD)
Liz - *Liz Amazing*
Jerry Neal - *I Love RV Life*
Brian (Tito) Pursel - *RV with Tito*
Jacob Rigor - *Rigor RV Repair*

A special thanks to Arlington RV Supercenter, Inc. in Rhode Island - to their team in general and especially to Tom Donnelly and Justin Rabideau in the service department, for bailing me out time after time after I've screwed up again.

PREFACE

Scientists say the Earth is comprised of neutrons, protons and electrons. They forgot morons.

You may decide I've proved the point after reading about my decades of RV camping. If you finish this book and conclude, *"this guy's a dingbat,"* at least give me that some of my blunders will ring familiar to folks who, like me, consider several TVs, a cushy mattress, and an electric fireplace to be about as "wilderness" as camping should get.

A note from my cover-your-behind department: I make no claim to technical expertise about RV's. I'm surely no Todd Henson whose helpful National RV Training Academy videos (NRVTA) are a wonderful resource on YouTube.

I'm handy with a computer but not so much with a wrench or a multimeter. If in doubt about something technical I mention, ask your dealer. That said though, if you discover a technical error herein, I'd sure love to know so I can make a correction.

Finally, I expect to make "bupkis" from this book - that's zilch, nada, zero. But if I sell even one copy, my vast riches won't come because I mentioned a product or service I was paid to push. That's not happening.

LET'S GET TO IT

WHEN J. K. ROWLINGS DECIDED to write the Harry Potter series, she sat down, grabbed a stack of paper napkins, a pen, and she outlined the plot for all seven novels. Folks like her amaze me for their ability to plan. But that's not me. I'm a dive-in and hope there's water in the pool kind-a-guy. It keeps life exciting, but it often leaves me two colors short of a full box of crayons.

Planning matters - especially in RVing. Mapping routes, identifying where to stop overnight, and what sights are must-sees, is all part of the fun. There's excellent software – some of it free - to help us plan and budget our daily travel progress. Pros offer "how to" videos on YouTube with technical tips to avoid misadventures along the way.

I'm not one of those pros, and after decades of RVing, I could fill a book with what not to do. So, I did. Write me off as a bad role model, but allow that every goof-up taught me something. So the following pages are an encyclopedia of "don'ts." (Not that anyone checks their encyclopedias anymore.)

RVing was not my first addiction. My love of the open road began as a kid in Michigan around the time Ben Franklin flew kites. Well, maybe I'm not quite that old, but it was back when a boy could get a driver's license at age fourteen. At 8 A.M. the morning of my birthday, I stood waiting to get in to our Town Hall, excited to take the driver's test.

I began my travels with a motor scooter that I drove all over Michigan. At sixteen I moved up to heavier iron - a motorcycle. At eighteen I traveled to London, bought a beat-up James motorcycle for a hundred bucks and motored on to Madrid, Lisbon, Rome, Munich and Paris. Yup, I roared through Europe on all the power its tiny 125cc engine could provide. (Actually, though the engine would be considered barely adequate for a moped these days, it was standard power for many motorcycles back then.)

We slept under bridges to save cash, visited Pamplona where the running of the bulls takes place, rode down the coast of Portugal from La Coruña, Spain and froze in 15-degree weather riding along the Brenner Pass between Austria and Italy.

Later boats became my fascination, fishing for striped bass and blues in the Atlantic off Long Island. I gravitated to airplanes, earning my pilot's license, then moving up the ladder to get a variety of ratings culminating in a twin-engine instrument sign-off before I hung up my headphones. (A minor medical issue kicked me out of the wild-blue-yonder.)

Then RVs became my passion, and they still are. I consummated my first love (a rig, not a "she") by signing a contract for a brand spanking new Class A Winnebago Adventurer. Back then, my boomer buddies looked down their noses at RVers as "trailer trash." Nowadays you'll find rock stars and even a Supreme Court Justice behind the wheel of a fancy Class A motorhome.

Before ordering the Winnebago, my wife and I rented a 35-foot Bounder as a test. We visited friends for a weekend, and I found maneuvering the big rig easy. My buddy, Art, with a great sense of humor, erected a 15-foot-high cardboard archway over his driveway and lettered it "RV CAMP." He lit it with strings of colored lights to welcome us to our first RV "park."

My version of scaling the Himalayas is climbing a couch, and since the Bounder came with a TV, I didn't have to miss the fall football games. Art's kids explored the rig, impressed that it had a bathroom, a bedroom and a kitchen all on wheels. They watched me in awe as I did my best Ali Baba impersonation and bellowed, *"Open Sesame,"* and the walls slid out to enlarge the living room.

My wife Susan and I enjoyed our first RV weekend enough to go to a Long Island dealer and order the Winnebago Adventurer built to our specifications. Susan picked from sheets of gaudy interior fabric. I was indifferent to decor but definite about the gold exterior paint I chose from a sheet of chips.

(The dealer said the Adventurer was a "Class A." A total newbie, I had no idea what RV class designations meant. I figured I must be getting a good one, not knowing that the class of RV has nothing to do with manufacturing quality or brand status. He later explained that the class identifies the type of "rig" - for example that Class A is a bus-like motorhome, and they can span the spectrum for price, quality, and length.)

Before our new motorhome arrived from the factory, someone told me I should tow a car. It would make it easier to get around once the coach is hooked up at a camp. "You don't want to have to hook up and unhook the power, water, and sewer every time you decide to go out to dinner or need a quart of milk," they explained.

I had a Saturn View at the time and purchased a Blue Ox tow package with the appropriate base plate for the car.

On the day of delivery, the dealer walked me out to my rig which towered like a Greyhound Bus. I hooked the Saturn up to it, jumped in the coach and drove away, not sure why the dealer looked bewildered.

Months later, returning to get my first dent repaired, the dealer remarked, "We were kind of surprised that you took off like that. We never got to show you how to use your rig."

"Gee, I never thought to ask," I said.

As a student pilot I spent hours training for my private license and for each rating above it. I'll never forget my first solo flight or the panic that set in as the wheels rose off the runway.

Could I get back on the ground? I mean, in one piece. Did I remember anything?

I don't know why I was cavalier about my first motorhome "solo". Maybe it's because there is no such thing as an RV license... even to drive the longest coaches. I guess I took comfort in knowing the Winnebago was unlikely to leave the ground. I got the coach home without issue, though my failure to ask questions didn't help my learning curve.

Speaking of learning curves: an RV is a house mated to a vehicle. Many RVs have a furnace, air conditioning, rows of plumbing pipes, miles of wires, more than one electrical system, and some have a generator or a solar system, or both. RVs travel on tires (or are carried on tires in the case of a truck camper). They have engines or are towed by a truck with one. The point is that RVs combine the complexity of a house plus a vehicle.

Today's autos are complicated enough. You need a degree in Dashboard-ology. Car insurance is skyrocketing in part because makers keep adding computers, chips and buttons. It's why the day you pick up your new car, the salesman sits with you and takes you through an array of features. For an RV, the need to learn them is tenfold.

Remember when you bought your first home. Before you signed that foot deep stack of papers, you had a "walk-through." A pro checked out your home.

Because you're a better planner than I am, when you buy an RV, you definitely want a "walk-through." Estimate the time you think you'll need to get familiar with the features in your RV - then double it. I wish I'd asked my salesperson to show me each system in the RV. Now I'd arrive with a checklist of questions and ask for hands-on instruction for every feature.

Imagine your frame-of-mind during the RV "walk-through." There she is - your new (or used) RV - gleaming in the sun. You're hypnotized by the fancy LED under-the-counter, color-changing lights or the push-button, heated lounge chair, or a solar system that displays incoming watts. Do you think you're going to remember all you're being shown?

Get out your smartphone and video the whole "walk-through." For example, if the rig has a command center, record the explanation of what each icon controls. Record how to operate the automatic leveling system. Even experienced RVers find bells and whistles that are new to them. If you're a newbie, don't be intimated or afraid to ask really basic questions. Get into the weeds. I wish I had, like:

How do you hook the power cord to the RV park's pedestal? Is surge protection important? How do you level the rig, and why does a propane refrigerator need to be on level footing? What difference does it make if the campground provides 30-amp or 50-amp service? Does it affect your use of appliances? Where's the fuse box? And when the lights go out – and they will someday – where's the GFCIs (ground fault circuit interrupters), and which area does each one control? Do you need a generator? Can it run your air conditioning? What's a "soft start"? How do you hook to city water? To park sewer? How do you find a dump station? How do you read grey and black tank levels? Does it matter which tank you empty first? What's a black tank clean-out port? Is there an alert if the propane leaks? A CO_2 detector?

Boondocking? What the hell is a "boondock." Do ships anchor in RV camps?

The list of newbie questions should be lengthy because RVs aren't simple. Experienced RVers have a lot of the answers, but even they need to ask about features that differ model to model and maker to maker. For example, the levers that redirect water flow for winterization may differ from RV to RV.

A good dealer will appreciate your questions and enjoy answering them. Others will get impatient, try to hurry you along, or tell you to find it in the owner's manual. If you get attitude, hopefully you've retained the option to vote with your feet.

Ideally the dealership has a full hook-up on site so you can test everything - the electrical systems, the plumbing for the sink, shower, toilet, the black and grey tanks and the outside shower wand. Test the appliances. Push every button. You're likely to discover some defects. You may not find them all, but you'll find some.

Spend the night camping in the rig, and ask the dealer to block service time for repairs before you leave his lot. (Don't plan your overnight on a Friday if the service department is closed on Saturdays.)

But I'm ahead of myself. Before we learn about how the RV operates, we need to get one.

The RV for You

SCORES OF YOUTUBE VIDEOS DESCRIBE the benefits of each different Class of RV. They give the pros and cons of specific manufacturers, describe options, and pick the ideal room layout. But there isn't a "right" layout. You wouldn't say a townhouse is better than a single family or that a modern decor beats colonial every time. All that matters is your family's needs.

Take it from a guy who never won a prize for thoughtfully choosing his RVs. My pulse would start racing the minute I stepped in a rig and saw a state-of-the-art stainless-steel kitchen, or when I watched a flashy TV screen rise from the counter on a Televator. Wiser today, before I let myself swoon at full body paint or ogle color-changing under-the-counter LED lights, I remind myself why I travel and who comes along. It inoculates me against love at first sight.

Charlie Brown would never leave without his security blanket. I can forget to pack socks or shirts, but I always bring an obsessive amount of electronic paraphernalia - every imaginable computer accessory with a plug or a cable. Should the apocalypse occur while I'm out camping, I'm able to supply anyone left during doomsday with every chord, plug, hub, cable, line extender, USB adapter, monitor, stand, web cam, portable scanner, printer or any other gadget they might need. There may be no electricity left in the world, but I'll have the plugs.

The point is that my addiction to cords ought to impact my choice of RVs. For example, I need desk space more than I need a bunkhouse. Your needs are different.

My third RV was a 24' Class C Phoenix Cruiser purchased slightly used. It was well-priced, low-mileage and it gleamed. It was gold, and I'm a sucker for gold paint. The problem was, it wasn't a smart buy *for us.* As we barreled down the highway, my wife would remind me that the space wasn't adequate for all my computer paraphernalia, our two dogs, and our habit of spending more time on Netflix than on a woodland trail. The Phoenix had a couch you had to remake into a bed, and Susan got tired of having to pull it open and make up the bed several times a day. I had fallen in love with a "deal" that was the wrong deal for us.

Each RV Class Type has virtues and shortfalls. I find Class A, B and C motorhomes easier to maneuver than a pull-behind trailer or a 5th wheel. But that maneuverability is offset by the fact that if you don't tow a car, you have to bring in your connections at the campground if you want to leave to shop, to visit local attractions, or to try that restaurant a campground neighbor said was good. The virtue of 5th wheels is that once you arrive, unhitch and setup, you're free to leave your rig hooked up and drive off. That's true of Class As, Bs and Cs too - as long as you tow.

Do you tend to extend stays at an RV park, or do you move on daily? If you do a lot of one-nighters, maybe a motorhome without a tow car isn't right for you. Maybe a Class B isn't right for the same reason. Setting up and tearing down at each campground is time-consuming, and it's really annoying after you've just hooked up and realize you need a quart of milk.

We rarely travel with kids or grandchildren. You may do so often. So how many beds or bunks will you need? There are dozens of rig designs to consider as you plan.

If you plan to boondock, there's a new set of questions. Does the rig you're considering have holding tanks adequate for your typical length-of-stay. Will power come from a generator, and will it run on propane, gas or solar? What kind of batteries are ideal and what's your budget for them? Some families outline their needs well. Impulse buyers like me need to walk into the dealership with a list.

The price range for Class A motorhomes runs from modest to Midas. High end coaches like a Prevost can cost millions. And yes, that "s" on the end of million is for real. One under construction for a customer right now will hit a price near three million dollars.

I may drool when I stand at the side of an ultra-luxury, super-expensive motorhome. But one look at its wiring gives me heart fibrillations. We're talking miles not yards of wires that require specialized troubleshooting when something goes on the fritz – and something always will. Class A, B and C motorhomes have engines to maintain. Class B's have the highest cost per square foot. Class C's often provide space at comparatively reasonable costs. What's the right rig for you?

Have a Pro Check it Out - New or Used

YOU WOULDN'T BRING A MECHANIC to a new car dealer's show-room. You assume everything works. And if a problem crops up, the manufacturer's warranty or a recall will set it right.

Sorry, but that's not how it is if you're buying an RV. A better mindset is to think about buying a home. Before closing, you hire a professional home inspector. The specialist goes through the house - roof to basement - and produces a detailed report covering the issues that ought to be addressed.

That prepurchase inspection is essential when you buy an RV. What folks new to RVing may not know it that the inspection is every bit as important when you're buying a brand new RV. Why? Because especially for a rig manufactured during or post COVID (when parts shortages resulted in "creative" substitutions), manufacturing issues abound. New or used, you want a pro to go through the rig.

Examples? Creative part substitutions have included screws that are too short or too long (or that are missing entirely) and have resulted in leaks and even fixture separations. There are issues with frames that flex, crack and cause havoc with a rig. The plumbing can have issues. Electrical issues may crop up when you test. New isn't perfect in RV-Land, and a used RV could be available because the previous owner dumped his headaches.

I found a ten-year-old, low-mileage 35-foot Thor Chateau at a bargain price. The engine was smooth and the tires had deep tread. What I didn't know but learned on my maiden voyage was that tire age is as important as tread depth.

Though little used, the Chateau's black and shiny tires were a decade old. Sure enough, South along I-95 - BANG. A tire blew and sent rubber flying like shrapnel. It tore off some side molding and severed a wire to some of the rig's lighting.

I limped off the expressway and found a wonderful tire company - the Manning Tire Company in Fayetteville, N.C. They stocked the replacement tire and had me back on the road quickly. But the importance of tire age is branded in my mind.

I didn't know that RV tires have lifespans that differ from car tires. I think about replacing my car's tires sometime after they hit thirty or forty thousand miles. Tire wear for an RV is typically viewed in years – often calling for replacement after three or four years. Many are considered unsafe after five years of use.

I knew little about roof maintenance and delamination. To me, the Chateau's roof looked "white and shiny." Who knew that even a small imperfection on the roof could create an opening for water to get in and travel along the sides of a rig.

It wasn't long before bulges in the cap of the Chateau appeared like a teenager's pre-prom pimple. Unlike acne, you can't buy cosmetic cream for RV roofs. *Cha-ching*

Think what a prepurchase inspection would have saved me, not to mention the time and aggravation waiting for parts and repairs.

(Note: I also didn't know that some RV parks won't accept reservations if the motorhome is ten years old or older. One park asked me to send photos to prove that my coach wouldn't make my campground neighbors think the *The Beverly Hillbillies* had come to visit.)

Under the Spell of the Gleam and Shine

I HAD OWNED A CLASS A and two Class C motorhomes by the time I decided to buy my fourth RV - a 5th wheel. I wanted to avoid the hassle of maintaining two vehicles that each had a motor. I also figured towing a 5th wheel with a truck rather than towing a car with a coach would improve my gas mileage.

As usual, I jumped in with both feet. I found a 35 foot Keystone Cougar 5th wheel from a dealer outside Buffalo, New York who advertised it at the lowest price I'd seen.

In a highly competitive market, RV inventory levels fluctuate. When lots are full, dealers often advertise RVs at promotional prices "near cost." The same goes for RV shows where discounted specials are described as at "dealer cost."

I bought the rig at close to dealer cost, but the good deal I got was more of an accident than due to shrewd negotiation. I'd planned to pay cash rather than finance - simply because I didn't want debt. I wasn't aware that the dealer expected to make up for the low price with what he'd earn selling a loan. RV dealers are like bankers in that a significant portion of their profit comes from selling finance packages and extras.

I rarely buy extended warranties and kept saying "No thanks" to each option the aggressive Business Manager offered. His face grew increasingly annoyed as the paperwork progressed, but I ended up purchasing at a rock-bottom price. Before patting myself on the back, stay tuned. I would wipe out what I saved by how poorly I planned for the day I picked up my rig. More about that soon.

I needed a truck to tow the 5th wheel, and my local Ford dealer sold me a new Ford F-150 – a half ton with a short bed. I'd given him the 5th wheel's specs, and he said the F-150 could handle the 11,000-pound rig. In retrospect, I don't think either of us had a clue what those specs meant. I wanted to save money, and a half-ton truck cost less.

The F-150 did tow the 5th wheel easily, and it was safe as far as the rig's weight in the truck bed. Braking was another matter. The half-ton needed considerable distance to stop the heavy rig, and I found myself perpetually alert to how much length I'd need to stop safely. It's a habit that saved my life as you'll see.

I needed a hitch to attach the new 5th wheel to the truck. My RV dealer at home installed one in the truck bed, but they couldn't set the height of the hitch without having the RV. I knew nothing about hitches let alone that they adjust to match the pin height on the 5th wheel.

Hindsight is perfect, but if I could rewind the tape, I'd order my truck from a local dealer with a history of selling trucks for use with RVs.

I'd buy the RV locally as well and have the RV dealer install the hitch and a brake controller (if needed as an aftermarket item) in the truck. If I had done it that way, I'd have avoided the costs that were about to hit me for doing things like a novice - assbackwards.

I wouldn't buy a half-ton truck. Two years later, having owned my 5th wheel a while, I ordered a Ford F-250 – a three-quarter-ton truck built with the largest V8 gas engine and the maximum tow capacity available from Ford for a F-250. I found helpful charts online that gave the tow capacities by truck brand based on a variety of setups. I took the chart to my Ford dealer, asked for the gear ratio that provided the maximum tow capacity, and I ordered the heavy duty tow package with bed holes pre-drilled for the hitch.

The heavier F-250 makes towing and especially stopping easier. Adjusting the factory brake controller is simpler than the aftermarket unit I'd put in the F-150. I ordered gas vs. diesel and I'm fine with that decision. A mistake I made was that I should have ordered the larger capacity gas tank so I cold stop for fuel less often.

If I buy a third truck someday, I'll order a Ford F-350 - or the RAM or GMC equivalent. A one-ton would let me upgrade to a longer, heavier 5th wheel should I choose to. I might even order the

F-450 which has a tighter turning radius than the F-350. I feel like I'm steering an Abrams tank when I struggle to get the F-250 into a parking lot at a crowded supermarket. (Not that I've ever driven an Abrams. I couldn't afford the fuel.)

Many Ford trucks came with a Pro Trailer Backup Assist system. It lets you position your trailer while you back up by steering with a knob on the dash. The system takes significant setup and doesn't work with 5th wheels, but it's worth checking out if you tow a pull-behind.

I agree with the sage advice offered on *Liz Amazing's* YouTube channel. Liz favors buying the RV near home even if it means you pay more. The convenience of staying local for service issues and warranty work is worth a premium, and will save you money in the long run.

YouTube has more than a few videos featuring buyers forced to drive their brand new rig long distances back to their dealer and even to the manufacturer for repairs. Often they have to leave the rig for weeks at a time and travel back and forth multiple times.

Life is too short for that kind of hassle.

"Sign Here" For Your New RV

AFTER YOU FALL IN LOVE with a shiny rig, there's the standard RV Purchase Agreement. The dealer sticks page after page in front of you and says, "Sign by the X."

Among my occupational past lives, I was the VP of Marketing for a cruise line. Let me assure you, the lawyers who wrote Maritime Law didn't create the small-print to protect the passenger. Their aim was to build a legal fortress to shield ship owners from liability, and when you buy a cruise ticket, you've agreed to their terms.

Likewise, RV sales contracts and manufacturer warranties weren't written for us. A team of toss-them-raw-meat lawyers sat around to strip buyers of rights that ought to be sacrosanct. All fifty states have lemon laws to protect consumers from poorly manufactured cars. But at this writing *only seven states include motorized RVs in their lemon laws.*

You can watch hours of YouTube videos with horror stories about innocent buyers who plead with the manufacturer to buy back a poorly constructed, sometimes unusable new rig - or at least, for example, to fix the frame flex - or the delamination after the roof leaked and blistered the coach. I'm talking about rigs that are new from the factory. Watch the *Liz Amazing* YouTube channel, but have a stiff drink nearby. The bottom line is *caveat emptor.*

Which gets us to the frame-of-mind we're in as we're led into the Business Mangers office. We're excited to take ownership of a new rig. Psychologically, the scale is loaded in the dealer's favor as you're handed sheet after sheet to sign. The experience can be overwhelming and as with the back of your telephone bill, what buyer reads the small print?

Follow the Boy Scout motto and be prepared. Think back to the last car you bought. The dealer handed you a contract and suddenly transport charges and dealer prep costs ballooned the amount you thought you were paying.

You were urged to add tire insurance, extra paint protection or an extended warranty. RV dealers share in the finance profits on loans that can last 10-15 years, and some run to 20. Seventy percent of buyers finance their RV, and of those, *90% never shop for financing alternatives*. Explore financing options before you walk you into the RV Business Manager's office.

Before you bought, you probably considered buying used vs. new. In RV-land, new isn't always safer, and rigs depreciate faster than cars. New doesn't eliminate risk just as used could land you with a lemon somebody unloaded. But on the pro side for a used rig, many older rigs were constructed to stricter standards using higher-quality materials. As noted before, it's so important to hire a pro to evaluate the rig you're considering - new or used.

New Doesn't Mean It Works

I'D HEARD A FOLK TALE about a fellow who drove a motorhome towing a car up a steep mountain road. In the sideview mirror, he saw a car like his trying to pass.

He pointed it out to his wife. "That's a car just like ours."

As the story goes, it *was* his car which had broken loose from the hitch. They watched it proceed on its own over the mountain cliff.

The story sounded far-fetched until the day we were en-route to attend a funeral in Vermont in our motorhome and towing the Saturn View. I heard an odd noise from the rear of the coach and pulled over.

Standing at the back bumper, I discovered that our Saturn was trying to pass us on the left. Half of the motorhome's hitch had swung out from the bumper. I disconnected the Saturn, and my wife and I drove home separately. We missed the funeral which, had the Saturn View broken fully loose, could have been for us or some poor soul approaching from the other direction.

After inspecting the rig, our dealer explained that the motorhome's hitch has a bar that runs beneath the bumper. That bar is attached by two bolts - one at either end. The factory had installed only one of the two bolts which allowed one end of the bar to swing out from the bumper with the car attached. No manufacturer is perfect. That's why there's recalls.

Sometimes factory specifications are themselves in doubt. We were headed home from Florida northbound a few miles from the George Washington Bridge. If you've ever crossed the GW bridge, you know the approach is one of the most congested, pothole-riddled roads in the Northeast.

Passing drivers were waving and pointing to our rig – the dreaded alert. As soon as I found a little space on the side of the interstate, I pulled over.

The 5th wheel came with a fancy storage rack that pulls out over the bumper on rails. The rack had bent and was dragging and sparking on the highway. The owner's manual rates the rack's carrying capacity at several hundred pounds. Ours carried only a small generator and a light aluminum ladder – totaling about half the rated carry weight.

Keeping an eye on semis whizzing by just feet from me, I removed the generator and the ladder and set them inside the 5th wheel. I bent the rack up enough to get it off the highway so we could limp back to Rhode Island to my RV dealer.

The 1st corollary of Murphy's law is that it applies anytime it can, and it did. The manufacturer doesn't sell parts for the rack. The rails and rack had to be removed and a whole new unit installed. *Cha-ching.* (I no longer trust the rack's advertised weight capacity, and I won't extend it on the rails again.)

Hitch? What Hitch?

I'M NOT SURE IF THIS one's on the hitch manufacturer or on me, but let me tell you of the *mystery of the missing hitch*. I should have asked Sherlock Holmes to ride along and help me solve it.

I towed the 5th wheel twelve hundred miles from Rhode Island to Southern Florida. On arrival at our park, I unhitched for the night. The next morning I climbed into the truck bed to get a suitcase only to find that the entire top half the hitch was missing. I was staring at a hitch base that didn't have a top portion with the arms that secure the pin.

I found it. There it was on the floor of the bed near the cab - completely off the base. The bolts that secure it had worked out. To this day I don't know how we made it safely to Florida.

More recently, returning from Maine to Rhode Island, while unpacking on arrival, I found one of the two massive side bolts that hold the hitch laying on the bed floor. It's a newer hitch, and if I'd paid attention and followed the manual carefully, I'd have seen that proper maintenance includes checking and re-torquing the bolts frequently (as with the lug nuts on tires). I got lazy and I didn't, which, as they say on cigarette packs, can "be hazardous to your health."

When It's the Park, Not the Rig

DEALERS, MANUFACTURERS AND DRIVERS MAKE mistakes, but RV parks aren't perfect. I arrived at a campground just after having the converter box in my motorhome replaced. When I plugged into the camp's 50-amp pedestal, the rig was dead – no 240v power.

I assumed my RV dealer must have installed the new converter incorrectly and called them. They had me test the GFCI boxes and a few other things, and then suggested, "Unplug from the pedestal's 50-amp socket and try the 30-amp socket."

Sure enough, as soon as I did, we had power. Faulty wiring at the pedestal's socket was the culprit. Naive, I'd assumed there couldn't possibly be a problem with the campground's equipment.

Now I use a Watchdog surge protector. I like it a lot because it instantly tests the camp's power before I hook power to my rig. Faulty power has ruined more than a few RVer's holiday. The Watchdog's face turns white if the camp's power is safe, red if its service fails the variety of tests it runs.

Another campground installed their pedestal on a post so low to the ground that the only way I could get my Watchdog surge protector plugged in and connected to my RV's power cable was to twist the Watchdog's thick cord up way more than I wanted to. When I got it attached, I couldn't raise it much, and in heavy rains it had to lay on the ground as a puddle grew. I tried to wrap it in plastic, but I worried water might still get into the plug. It didn't, but I'm guessing the wizard who installed the box on such a short post doesn't RV much.

How Not to Pick Up Your New RV

AFTER DECIDING TO GO FROM a motorhome to a 5th wheel, and agreeing on terms with the dealer, we headed to Buffalo to get my new rig. Murphy (the lawmaker who invented chaos) decided it was time for a full-blown Buffalo snowstorm with inches of white stuff hurling off Lake Erie. On arrival at the dealership, I was anxious to hit the road with the rig for the eight-hour trip home to Rhode Island.

Standing in the dealer's bay beside my new 5th wheel, I didn't ask many questions. I was worried about the storm and not able to concentrate. What's more, I didn't know what to ask. I watched the dealer secure the 5th wheel pin to the hitch in the Ford F-150, plug in the 7-pin power line and attach the breakaway cord, and then I headed off into a sea of white.

A few miles from the dealership, clearly something wasn't right. Each time I applied the brakes, the rig bucked like a skittish horse. I pulled over and with snow piling on my windshield, I called the dealer.

"You need to adjust the brake controller," he said.

"What's a brake controller? I asked.

"Oh that," I said remembering the box under the truck's steering column installed by a dealer back home. The Buffalo dealer talked me through how to alter its sensitivity. I wasn't good at it, but I reduced the bucking from a snake-scared mustang to a jumpy pony.

Give Me a Brake

I LEARNED QUICKLY THAT TOWING WITH a half-ton truck requires paying extra attention to stopping distance - a habit that saved my life.

We were returning from Florida, towing the 5th wheel on a multi lane highway about ten miles south of the infamous Washington Beltway. I saw rows of taillights turn red ahead and started to slow. But two ying-yangs in cars on my left were paying no attention, probably texting, and kept roaring on. Both drivers finally noticed the danger at the same time and reacted by swerving into the same lane, same space. They crashed and sent fenders flying, and I mean it literally because a big fender flew over my windshield. They slammed into others and a multi-car pileup was underway.

Fifty yards dead ahead, an SUV spun around and came to rest sideways across my lane. If I did nothing, I'd hit it for certain. If I swerved and there was a car in the lane on my left, I'd hit it. But hitting it sideways might not be as bad as a direct hit to the SUV. This occurred in an instant of course, and I had no time to check traffic. So I swerved left and thankfully the lane was clear, and I was able to ease all 55 feet of my rig around the hood of the stalled SUV.

I didn't stop and kept working my way past a half-dozen cars that were spinning in all directions. Somehow, I made it through the crash scene unscathed. Half of it was luck, but paying constant attention to stopping distances gave "luck" a helping hand.

True Confessions: I Get Bent Out of Shape.

I SPEND A LOT OF TIME watching RV channels on YouTube. There's *All About RVs* with Jared Gillis, *Liz Amazing* whose advice I've mentioned, and Jason Epperson's *RV Miles* which is loaded with the solid industry news.

Another favorite channel is *Keep Your Daydream* (KYD) with Marc and Tricia Leach, although rumor has it that their program is secretly directed by their wonder dog, Charlie. (Well, maybe Charlie just shows up.)

But be careful if you watch *KYD*. You could become a foodie if you follow Tricia's cooking, or immerse yourself in their restaurant videos as they crisscross America in a variety of cool RVs. Marc and Tricia offer useful tips on RV ownership, and though Charlie doesn't have a lot to say, he's clearly celebrity material.

One bit of Marc's wisdom is worthy of the Dalai Lama.

When maneuvering your rig, remain in a state of peace. Don't let yourself be rushed. Slow is safe, slow is pro.

Ignore the crowd watching like judges at a county fair as you back into your site.

Many dents later, Marc's advice has become my motto. I repeat what he said and remind myself: *Go slow.* Unfortunately, I hadn't heard Marc yet the day I backed our new 35' Adventurer – our first RV – into a narrow, grassy park site.

My wife wasn't around to spot me. (A partner spotting via cell phone or walkie talkie can save the day – though it could send you to a marriage counselor). I didn't see an insolent rock that got aggressive with my rear storage compartment. The dent required a trip to our dealer and a thousand plus for the repair. Worse, the paint they used was a poor match and turned my one-tone rig into a two-tone.

The dent could have been avoided had I taken the time to hop out and walk around the rig a few times to check my progress. I'd have seen the rock. But I got lazy and relied on the passenger-side mirror which lacked the angle to show the rock. Lazy costs *beaucoup* bucks in RV-land.

A wiser though poorer man, more recently when I'm backing my truck to hitch up, or if I'm backing my rig to enter a site, I hop out even a dozen times if need be to check for poles, pedestals, water faucets, overhead tree limbs and other lurking obstacles. I feel like I've run a four-minute mile after the twelfth hop-in-hop-out of the cab, but my rig doesn't take a hit.

I Get Hitched

My introduction to hitch casualties occurred early in my 5th wheel days when I visited Cape Cod to give a talk on publishing. Backing the truck up to the pin, I shifted from reverse into park and jumped out to see how things were lining up. The shift didn't take because as I stood near the pin box, the truck began rolling towards my rig. I raced and dove into the cab to hit the brake, but my foot hit the gas instead. BANG.

That blunder sent my rig to the body shop for two months awaiting parts. A couple thousand dollars poorer and my ego also dented, I was, in the words of Willie Nelson, back on the road again. Now every time I shift into park while hitching up, before I hop from the cab, I say "PARK" out loud and check the dash to confirm the shift took. *He's talking to himself again*, my wife thinks.

With the 5th wheel, it might take me twenty minutes and a dozen tries to get the hitch hooks approaching the pin at the proper angle and height. (If you're new to a 5th wheel as I was, you can "over pin" or "under pin" if you don't latch the pin at the right height.)

Early in my 5th wheel days, I thought I had to slam the hitch into the pin. In time I learned to back the hitch to within an inch or two of the pin and then gently ease it into the hitch arms.

I screwed up another time hooking the hitch in my F-150 to the RV. Certain that I had secured the pin properly, I pulled forward a couple feet. CRASH. The pin flew out of the hitch, and the RV slammed down on the tailgate. Did someone mention *"pull test"*?

My F-150's tailgate now had a unique design similar to a musical instrument - the accordion. *Cha-ching.*

Now like a postman, neither rain nor snow nor dark of night will see me skip a pull test. And, as they say in infomercials, *"but wait... there's more."*

The next time I dropped the 5th wheel on the truck, I'd hitched properly and had done a proper pull test. But on leaving the lot where I store the RV, I turned at an almost 90-degree-angle. The rig rotated in the truck's short bed until it hit the back of the cab, and the pin came out of the hitch. CRASH *again*. The 5th wheel wasn't dented but the cab acquired a shape the Ford design studios never envisioned.

I'm still not totally sure why the pin came out, but the rig hit the cab because I hadn't paid attention to how tight I was turning in a short bed truck.

I waved goodbye to my 5th wheel as a tow truck carried it off to our body repair shop where, for obvious reasons, I'm considered royalty.

Two things have prevented this from happening again. I had the dealer install a "Reese Sidewinder" on the pin box. It's an arm that adds length between the pin and the hitch to provide extra bed clearance during sharp turns. When later I purchased the F-250, I ordered a longer bed. (Another way I could have addressed the problem was by installing a sliding hitch that rolls back on rails during turns to provide more clearance. But my Sidewinder does the trick.)

Currently I use a Curt hitch that displays a green circle if the hitch arms are secure around the pin. If they aren't, the circle shows red. Initially I had to climb in the bed to see what color the circle was. I bought a small hand-mirror at a dollar store and attached it to the end of an extendable selfie-stick. I slide the stick into the bed and can see the circle color without having to climb in.

I used to try to hook up in one run at the pin. Now I back up in small increments and get out often to check my approach angle to the pin and to raise or lower the RV for the right hookup height. Initially I bought a video camera specifically designed to let me watch my approach to the pin from inside the cab. I don't use it much anymore because I'm finally pretty good at hitching – *(I just cursed myself, didn't I?)*

For pull-behind RVs, the new Pebble Flow EV Trailer has a "Magic Hitch" that actually hitches itself to its tow vehicle using sensors. It's amazing and gives us a look at the future of travel trailers that will make life easer for many RVers.

I've never owned a tow dolly, deciding they were the least desirable tow option. As is also the case with a tow bar hitch, not every make and model car can be flat towed just as not all cars can be towed by a dolly. Loading and unloading a car on a dolly takes longer than hooking up a tow bar. A dolly adds length, and you're not supposed to tow in reverse using a dolly. There are also weight and vehicle make limitations for both four tires down or two up car dollies, and after you arrive and unhook, you have to store the dolly somewhere.

My Heroic Tire Rescue

Virginia boasts that it's "for lovers," but for us it's for tire issues. On another trip heading north after sun and fun in Florida, we ran into a blizzard outside of Richmond. Rather than bypass the city via its beltway, we opted for the road through downtown as it looked better plowed.

The Chateau motorhome's tires sport fancy, chrome wheel simulators. They're bigger than just a hubcap and mimic chrome wheel rims. Moving in heavy traffic, I heard a clang and looking back, I saw one of the simulators roll from its tire into lanes of speeding cars. The simulator came with the motorhome's wheels, and I dreaded replacing it if I could even find one.

I pulled the motorhome off the highway determined to do something though I wasn't sure what. With snow blowing and traffic whizzing by me, I waited for just the right moment. I dashed between spaces in the traffic, grabbed the heavy chrome simulator and carried my prize back to the rig. Miraculously neither of us got crushed.

I put the simulator back on when we got home and replaced the chrome-like nut covers that had also come off. My wife suggested that I value wheel decor more than my life. She had a point.

I did most of the driving, but on occasion Susan drove. We were South of Richmond Virginia in our Chateau motorhome, passing miles of road construction on I-95. Workers wearing yellow helmets stood along the highway staring at a stack of metal sign poles they had dropped in our lane. We were in the far-right lane, barreling straight for the poles, with cars on our left.

Susan screamed, "*I'm going to hit them. What should I do?*"

"*Keep going and run over them,*" I yelled, knowing if she swerved we'd hit a car.

Susan held the rig straight, ran over the stack of poles, braked, and slowly pulled off the highway. The construction workers were laughing, finding the whole thing amusing and not in the last concerned that they'd endangered us and others.

I hopped out to inspect the damage. The tires on the motorhome looked okay, but the front and rear passenger-side tires on our tow vehicle looked like peeled bananas. We called for a tow truck since the car couldn't be moved in that condition.

The driver had to load it on a platform and carry our Saturn View to the nearest dealer. Later that afternoon, with two new tires on our tow car and a two-page bill, we were back on the road.

I gave my wife repeated kudos for staying cool and for resisting the impulse to swerve to avoid the poles which would have resulted in a crash. I thought about complaining to the Virginia Highway Authority, but I never did.

If only that's how this episode ends, but it isn't. Further North the following day, the motorhome's right front tire wobbled flat. It developed a slow leak from passing over the poles. Another tow truck arrived to help remove the flat and put on the spare tire.

Knowing Murphy's fondness for chaos, I didn't want to risk traveling several hundred miles further without a spare, and the flat wasn't worth fixing. The driver recommended a nearby shop in Delaware where I bought another new tire. *Cha-ching*.

In Praise of Good Guys

Like most RVers, I've had to deal with flat tires. After a series of tires that turned to pancakes, I finally got a TPMS (tire pressure monitoring systems). It's an annoying, sometimes inconsistent accessory that suffers from hypochondria and complains a lot. But twice over the years it alerted me to a problem before my rig was at risk. I figure the only thing worse than having a nagging TPMS is not having one.

It's a chore to check tire pressure and be sure it matches the TPMS's reading. But I was glad I had my tire minder as we headed for a week of camping in Maine. It started beeping and flashing to warn that the right rear tire on the 5th wheel was losing pressure though it wasn't yet flat.

On the side of the highway, I took out my air compressor and spare car battery and refilled the tire. We continued on while my wife called every nearby tire company google could locate. It was Friday afternoon in Maine's vacation season, and everyone we reached was too jammed to take us, and several didn't service RVs. Meanwhile, I kept pulling off the road, stopping, dragging out my compressor and battery to refill the tire.

Not far from our campground destination, I saw a sign for Seacoast RV's, Inc. of Saco Maine. On a whim I pulled in and explained our predicament. Though it was late on a Friday afternoon, a friendly woman at the counter said she was sure they would help.

In no time their busy service manager had us move the rig around back to their service bays. He sent a man out who pulled, plugged and remounted the tire in minutes. I asked for the bill and was told it was on the house. I said that wasn't acceptable and insisted on paying for their time and kindness.

"Well, if you want, give a few bucks to my service guy who did the work," he said. And of course I did.

We hear about uncaring RV dealers and poor service, but please remember that there are a lot of Good Samaritan dealers like Seacoast RV out there. You can bet I left a glowing 5-star review for them on Google. It only takes a minute.

Mobile RV Support

Speaking of RV service people... I've used mobile service technicians to mixed reviews. Some were great – some so-so – one was a Grand Canyon's depth below acceptable. (More about him soon, but for the moment let's focus on a good one.)

A Good Samaritan technician helped us on a trip to Florida after I'd gone far enough south to de-winterize at a camp along the route. I hooked to the park's city water and tested the plumbing. Happily I'd winterized properly at the end of last season, and there were no leaks. But when I fired up the hot water heater, no matter what I did, all I could get was lukewarm water. I tried switching from propane to electric to heat the tank. Still, all we got was tepid water.

I called my RV dealer who had me check a few things including how I'd positioned the winterizing levers. He confirmed I had them in the proper positions. The hot water tank's propane was igniting and staying lit, so they were baffled too.

I found the Southern Mobile RV Service on google and called them. Over the phone, a friendly woman who totally knew her RVs, wanted to ask some questions before she sent a technician.

"Your rig has an outside shower?"

"Yes."

"Please check to make sure the shower knobs are in the fully off position."

I checked and sure enough, when I'd winterized at the end of previous season, I hadn't turned the cold-water knob to off. Cold water was still mixing with the system's hot water which is why it never got hot.

Despite my plea, this super-smart mobile tech person would not charge my card. The least I could do was to leave Southern Mobile a glowing 5-star review on Google – and you can bet I did.

But Baby It's Cold Outside

You know I'm no mechanical wizard, so when it was time to winterize, I'd have it done by a dealer. That meant that each time I left Florida to return north in the winter, I had to find a dealer along our route, make a service appointment, and wait at the dealership. After years of that, I wondered if I could do it myself. I know, for many this is child's play.

I learned how to position the water flow levers and remove the anode tube from the water heater to drain the tank. After draining the water and flushing the tank, I bought a small hand pump and sucked RV antifreeze through the pipes. I did okay and each time I de-winterized in the following season, there were no leaks.

I made one mistake. I forgot to first release the pressure value at the top of the water heater before unscrewing the anode tube. When I unscrewed it, under pressure, the anode tube shot out like a bullet. Happily, it only hit my heavy coat, but it could have done worse. That's another mistake I won't make again.

When I read up on how to winterize, I learned of a unit called the Floë Induratec System – a Lippert product. If you asked me what's the single best accessory I've ever found for an RV – this is it, and it's not well known.

The Floë is a lightweight, air compressor system added to your rig's plumbing. It winterizes by forcing air through the pipes to flush water out. I had my RV dealer install it, and it's simple to use. You flip a valve so the Floë is connected to all your pipes, and you switch it on.

You go to each faucet – one at a time - and open it – for example, first the cold, then the hot water knob. When you turn a faucet on, the Floë automatically sends compressed air through the related pipes. The water spits out until the Floë stops cranking, and it's loud. It stops when the pipe is free of water. You do this at each fixture

- including the toilet, the shower, the outside shower wand if you have one, and the water drain tubes under the rig. And that's it. In fifteen minutes, you're winterized. (As a double precaution, I pour a little RV-safe anti-freeze in the drains, shower and the toilet.)

My Problem Passing Gas

Maneuvering for fuel at stations brings challenges. I'm paranoid about running out of gas in my RV, and I start looking for a station when the gage dips below half-full. (I'm not mentioning my wife's tentative bladder because I need to live long enough to finish this book.)

If your fuel is diesel, truck stops are easy. Truck stops have long, dedicated fuel lanes for big rigs. But my fuel is gas and only a few stations have dedicated gas lanes for RVs, so maneuvering to get to the pumps can be tricky.

Marc Leach's advice that "slow is pro" applies tenfold at fuel stops. Before I enter a station, I scout out an exit route. If I don't see one that works for my RV, I'm off to another station.

I look for a pump I can successfully approach given 55 feet of truck and RV (or the same length when I had my motorhome towing a car).

Will I have enough room for the turn when I exit? Are there cars parked in front of the convenience store that will block my exit?

If there's a road that goes around the back of the station's convenience store, I'll often walk it to see if I can use it to exit. No one wants to unhitch just to get gas, although several folks on You-Tube say they've had to.

Fueling at service plazas along major highways presents a different challenge for long RVs. The newer plazas place the pump bays at angles. The layout may accommodate more cars, but it doesn't leave a lot of room for a big RV to squeeze in to a pump slot. In addition, semis often park along the exit road next to those pumps, further narrowing the approach for large RVs. Often a portion of a long RV is left sticking out into the exit road.

So we pump while praying that we're not blocking traffic. (When available, the first or the last pump in those rows seems to provide the widest space to swing as we exit.)

To reduce how frequently I have to stop for fuel, I wish I had opted for the larger gas tank when I ordered my Ford F-250. Some RVer's replace a standard factory gas tank with a larger aftermarket unit. Others install a second tank in the truck bed with a fuel transfer system.

(It's human to complain about the price of gas, but I remind myself that the cost of filling up is relative. An acquaintance who owns a large yacht spends a couple of thousand dollars to fill up. I picture him explaining to his bank manager that he needs a home loan line of credit is so he can fuel his boat. I suspect even owners of deluxe 45 foot motorhomes blink a few times when they see the total at the pump.)

Since this book could have been titled, *Confessions of a Wayward RVer*, it's time to "tell all" about my most expensive fuel stop. I paid about $50 a gallon if you count what this screw up cost me.

I entered the Maryland House Service Plaza along 1-95 towing my 5th wheel. The road forks at the entrance - one way for gas and another to park. I missed the fork for gas and needed to go around and reenter the plaza. To do so required a sharp left onto a narrow plaza exit road made even more narrow by an illegally parked semi.

Still, I estimated I had enough room and made a sharp turn at the curb. I misjudged it slightly, and the driver's-side wheel of my 5th wheel caught the curb. Normally, while undesirable, dragging my 5th wheel's tire slowly over a low curb wouldn't be worth a mention. But this curb was around a puddle that obscured a deep pit.

My rig's rear wheel rose gently over the curb but dropped into the pit. I was stuck, blocking the Southbound exit at a major interstate plaza. Intimidating semis big as mountains started lining up behind me.

I put my truck in reverse and rocked, but the tire would not climb out of the pit. I jammed it back and forth increasingly aggressively, until finally in a panic, I slammed it back over the curb. The driver in the parked semi gave me a guilty look and pulled away, knowing he shouldn't be there. Hindsight is perfect, and I could have politely asked him to pull ahead, but I didn't think of it in real time.

I freed the 5th wheel from the pit, but in doing so my rear electric leveling jack hit the cement curb and hung like a broken arm. *Cha-ching.* Hospitals dedicate wings to donors. Shouldn't my RV dealer dedicate a bay in my honor?

Backing Doesn't Always Get You Ahead

Before I bought my 5th wheel, I'd owned three motorhomes in succession. You can back up a 5th wheel or a "tow- behind," but motorhomes bring a special set of problems because they aren't meant to backup towing a car. The distance you can reverse without warping the tow bar is limited.

One "dark and stormy night" - to steal a mystery writer's cliché - I missed my turn to the interstate off a quiet country road. I was driving the motorhome and towing the Saturn View.

I drove on for several miles looking for a place to turn around. Not finding one, I decided to chance a U-turn. It was late and I hadn't seen a single car, so I swung the coach into the other lane. I got as far as the edge of a gully only a few feet short of the space I needed to complete the turn.

That's of course when a car approached from the other direction. I got nervous, but the kind driver in the approaching car stopped and waited. I had no choice but to slowly reverse for the extra feet I needed to finish my turn. By dumb luck when I checked the tow bar later, I hadn't bent it.

You may recall I hit a rock when I relied on my motorhome's side door mirror to back into a site. I dented my tow truck in another back-up accident by relying totally on my rearview mirror. Sideview mirrors carry a caution about perceiving distance, but a rearview mirror can be misleading also.

It looked to me like I had plenty of distance before I needed to hop out and drop my truck's tailgate. But I got too close and tapped the leading edge of the pin box. It was just a TAP, but I knifed a three-inch horizontal slice through the thin tailgate wall.

Murphy was there to be sure I sliced it in just the right place. I bent a lever that runs horizontally inside the tailgate from the handle to the release latch. We were about to leave for vacation, but now I couldn't open the tailgate and our suitcases were prisoners in the bed. My wife quipped that without a change of clothes, it would be a vacation to remember for anyone who got a whiff of us.

A rush to our Ford dealer followed, and though we didn't have an appointment, the busy service manager had mercy on us. With considerable difficulty they managed to fork a tool through the gash and release the tailgate. Once down, they took the tailgate apart, bent the lever back so the handle worked, and we were on our way. When we got back from vacation, the bodywork for the gash cost as much as the vacation. *Cha-ching.*

I was just as unlucky after I installed a Brake Buddy in my Saturn View. The Brake Buddy (required in Canada) is a robot-like assist box placed in the tow car. It has an arm that clamps on the pedal in the tow car and applies brakes whenever the motorhome's brakes go on.

I was leaving a parking spot, towing my Saturn View with the Brake Buddy turned on. I moved just a few feet forward before it was obvious that the RV wasn't moving easily. I thought, *I'll bet I left the Saturn's parking brake on,* and I got out to look. I hadn't.

Do you remember Hal from the *2001- A Space Odyssey* movie? Well, the Brake Buddy, in a moment of Hal-like robotic rebellion, decided to hit the brakes and lock the front wheels. I had only dragged the car a few feet - but it was enough to shred a tire. I do have this thing about tires, don't I?

If Only Columbus Had a Garmin

A GPS DESIGNED SPECIFICALLY FOR RV's is a fantastic tool. I'm in awe of the technology that maps roads world-wide and even keeps up to date with construction changes. Set up properly, the GPS routes you to avoid low bridges, parkways and roads that aren't RV-friendly. It helps you find a detour around accidents.

Besides mapping your route from A to B, having a GPS is like traveling with an attentive minion who sits on your dashboard and checks for gas stations, RV parks, repair mechanics, the nearest medical center, restaurants, banks, post offices, and of course, shopping. You can talk to your GPS, and it replies with its own voice commands which my wife says I obey better than her.

But even the best of them aren't perfect, (The GPS that is... wives are prefect.) On a trip to Vermont driving near Keene, New Hampshire, our GPS surprisingly directed us off the main highway and led us to a small, rural neighborhood.

If I could have held a complete conversation with our Garmin, it would have gone like this:

"Take a left at the traffic light," says Garmin.
"Are you sure this is right?" I asked.
"Not a *right*. I told you *left,*" It corrected.
"No, I mean is this the right route?"
"I said *left,*" It corrected again.
"But why are we leaving the main highway?" I asked.
"Just do as you're told," the GPS replied.
So I did.

But after the third round-trip around the same neighborhood block, it was obvious we weren't getting anywhere. Folks standing on their front porch began to wave, considering us old friends by now as our monstrous RV passed by – again. I finally abandoned the bossy GPS, relied on my sense of direction, and got us back to the interstate.

The RV GPS database is chock full of travel information, and as with any computer, the more you know about using it, the more useful it is. I'm on my third RV Garmin over many years, and I'm still discovering things I can do with it.

One thing apparently I haven't mastered is how to follow its "distance-to-turn" directions. The screen displays the distance to your next turn in descending fractions of a mile. Sounds simple, right? But sometimes the information is hard to interpret, and misinterpretation can lead to trouble.

One day in busy traffic, my GPS announced that my right turn was coming up. I was approaching two roads on my right, one immediately following the other. I saw no street signs, and the "distance-to -turn" on my GPS could apply to either road.

I took the first of the two. It turned out that the second road was the one the GPS wanted me to take. It didn't "recalculate" my route, and I assumed all was well - until it was too late. A half mile up the road I came to a dead end at a wall of cement construction barriers.

My truck and 5th wheel have a combined length of 55 feet. There was no way I could make a U-turn on the narrow road. I had two options, neither desirable. I could back up the 5th wheel for a half-mile on the curvy road with my wife walking beside and guiding me. Backing a 5th wheel into a camp site is hard enough. It's why folks want pull-through sites. To back a 5th wheel a half-mile, if I could do it safely along a two-lane road, would take hours.

My other option was a dirt road up a steep hill at the left of the construction barriers. I could enter the road and pull up just enough to gain room to reverse, then back down and complete a U-turn on the paved road.

I chose option two, pulled in and drove half our length up the steep hill. But when I began to back down to complete my U-turn, the hill was so steep that my back bumper dug in the soil. (The bumper carried a spare tire and the cover ripped as the bumper dragged the ground.)

Now all I could do was go forward. I didn't have a clue if I could make it up the hill or what I'd find if I did. I got out and walked up the hill. At the top was a construction site with men erecting a building. If I could make it up the hill with my rig, the worksite had enough room for me to turn around.

Workers stared in disbelief as 55 feet of truck and 5th wheel suddenly rose over the top of their hill. They stopped work and stared as I was able to turn around, head down, and handle the decent angle without getting stuck.

I was happily back on the highway - that I shouldn't have been on in the first place - thanks to misinterpreting my GPS.

Sea to Shining Sea in My RV

In flying, the pilot in command has the final say over even the control tower. If a pilot receives an instruction that he or she does not think is safe, it's the pilot's choice to obey it or not… though the pilot better be ready to justify the decision.

There's no such rule when it comes to RVing, but sometimes we're asked to do something that we ought to question. If it doesn't feel right, let someone know.

I was driving the 35 foot Chateau motorhome (towing the Saturn View) and waiting in a line of cars to board the Steamship Authority ferry from Woods Hole to Martha's Vineyard, Massachusetts. A high tide raised the angle of the ramp that brings vehicles into the ferry, and I was concerned that my motorhome's bumper might get stuck and drag at a point where the angle of the ramp was especially high. I talked to the crew member in charge of directing vehicles onto the ferry, and told him I didn't think I could make it.

He looked at my bumper and assured me, "You'll be fine. You have plenty of height." I didn't see it that way, but I figured, who was I to question a pro who boards big rigs all day long.

But sure enough, when he signaled our line of vehicles to proceed on board, *scrunch.* My bumper bottomed out on the ramp. I couldn't move forward or backward, and the Steamship Authority which prides itself on keeping on schedule, was about to lose time - big time.

Crew members gathered around my RV and scratched their heads. I suggested I could try to use the motorhome's hydraulic leveling leg to raise it. Then if the crew could support the bumper with lumber for just a little, I might be able to gain the inch or two needed to move past the high point. They told me to give it a try, I did, it worked, and we were soon safely on the ferry. When we debarked at

Martha's Vineyard, the descent angle wasn't a problem. But I should have trusted what I know about my rig.

Andy Warhol quipped that everyone gets fifteen minutes of fame. A ferry bound for Nantucket provided my brief moment in the spotlight.

This time when we were boarding, I was directed to drive the motorhome between two staggered rows of columns that ran the full length of the ferry. The columns were barely the motorhome's width apart, and I wasn't sure I had the room to pass. I pulled in my side mirrors, but it was still going to be tight.

Because the columns were staggered, the only way I could pass was to zig-zag - turning slightly left to get the mirror on the right around a column on the right, then slightly right at the next column to edge the driver's side mirror past the column. Susan confirmed at each column on her side that I had the inch to spare before I'd scrape.

When it was time to debark, by zigging and zagging, I made it the rest of the length to the end of the ferry. Word spread because passengers had lined up to witness me work my way along the columns. When I cleared the last one, folks started clapping and giving me a thumbs up. It gave me a moment's pride - though perhaps not enough to outweigh my decades of screw-ups.

Home on the Roadside

I've subscribed to roadside assistance plans and called for help several times when stuck on the side of a major highway. The best-known name among those plans failed to find help for us the two times I used them. On the other hand, National General, my RV insurance carrier, surprised me by finding someone quickly, and the wonderful lady called back repeatedly to be sure we were helped. She even insisted that my insurance would cover the service cost. Additionally, she stayed after her shift to be sure my issue was resolved.

I've relied on google to locate a nearby RV technician, and I've used the random techs they listed with mixed results. My worst mobile support experience happened on arrival at a campground in Florida. When our hot water heater wouldn't ignite, I located a mobile tech through google. The technician came, told me I needed a new water heater and gave me a price that was considerably higher than I expected. But we had just arrived to begin our vacation, so I said "okay." He promised to return the next day.

After three days of trying to track him down, he showed up and said he'd spent hours driving all over Florida to find a replacement water heater. (It was a common Suburban model.)

Once the new unit was installed, he handed me a bill for more than double his quote - about triple what I thought the job should cost. I argued. He hemmed, hawed and took a few dollars off. But in the end, I handed over my credit card.

Incidentally, when I needed to replace that same heater years later, I ordered it from Amazon. It arrived in three days and cost a fraction of what the mobile tech had charged. Like I say, some mobile services are great, and some - not so much.

I switched to CoachNet roadside service because their reviews were good. I've needed them twice, and both times they've been prompt to respond. They seem to have a broad network of RV repair technicians, and it helps that they are pleasant and call with status updates while you're anxiously waiting for help.

On one occasion, when I had an actual highway emergency, I called Keystone, the manufacturer of my 5th wheel. We were leaving a gas station in Ohio, entering a busy major highway with semis roaring by. At a pause in the traffic, I turned out onto the highway when - *screech* - my RV stopped dead. Approaching semis kept swinging to miss us.

I called the police for help, and they said they were on the way, but despite the "clear and present danger," they never showed. I also called Keystone the manufacturer and explained that all of a sudden my 5th wheel stopped dead in the highway, and I couldn't get it to move. Tech support had me check a few things, then told me to look at the emergency electric breakaway cord. (One end of the breakaway cord leads to a pull-out plug bolted to the pin box. The other I attach to a handle in my truck bed. In the rare event that the 5th wheel ever became disconnected from the truck, the plug gets pulled out which engages the brakes.)

Sure enough, the breakaway cord had caught the handle of my hitch. The cord pulled out during my sharp turn which activated the emergency brakes. I put the plug back in its socket which immediately released the brakes.

Thanks to that helpful Keystone technician, we were moving again and safe. It was a freak occurrence that's never happened again — but it got my attention. I've been mindful ever since to attach the breakaway cord to a place in the bed well clear of the hitch handle.

When Wi-Fi is No-Fi

For me, having usable internet when we camp is more important than hot water. (Please don't let Susan know I said this.) And when it comes to providing good internet, I've tried it all.

"Back in the day" as an RV newbie, campground brochures boasted free internet. I naively assumed that meant they had it. It took about two RV parks without getting emails before it dawned on me that campground Wi-Fi is as sure as a candidate's promise.

Some parks with "free" Wi-Fi charge an upgrade if you want a connection that's usable. Most of the parks with upcharges use third-party suppliers who provide a computer interface a NASA scientist couldn't decipher. You needed tech support to set it up, and good luck reaching tech support. What's more, they provided speed and data in step-up tiers at escalating prices. In decades of camping at scores of RV Parks, I've found usable, free Wi-Fi three times.

I tried to use my cell phone's hotspot which often provided adequate Wi-Fi, but data amounts were caped, and the charge for additional data was hefty. In marginal areas, I tried boosting reception with cellular amplifiers but found the equipment expensive and the benefit minimal.

I went on to purchase several dedicated hotspots. They provided adequate internet, depending on the cell service provider's coverage at each campground. But when cell coverage was marginal, the hotspots lacked antenna ports which would have helped boost reception.

Whatever cell carrier I used, I kept running into data limits, speed caps, or deprioritization. Once you hit a data cap, they cut speed so significantly that you can barely get an email, let alone stream TV.

One of the major cell service providers, besides charging heavily for extra data, advised me that after two purchases of more data in a month, I couldn't buy a third batch *at any price*. How weird is that?

For perspective, I'm not doing anything unusually data-intense. I'll host an occasional small zoom meeting – maybe twice a month. I stream a lot of TV news and Netflix, but it's not like I'm uploading hour-long YouTube videos.

After hotspots and cell boosters, I graduated to a cellular modem. The software interface to get it connected was above my pay grade, and I had to spend phone time with tech support to get online. Once it was set up, it worked well, and I could run an antenna to the modem for better reception.

Yet the data limit problem remained. I couldn't escape the reality that whatever sim card I inserted, I was still tied to the cellular service's data limits, to their upcharges for more data, or to their limit on how much data they would sell at any price.

My search for a viable connection continued, and I bought a satellite dish. Extras included a table to set the dish on, a longer cord, and a gage to help me aim at satellites. Finding satellites was time-consuming especially since we frequently spend a single night at campgrounds on route to our final destination. Each stop meant moving the dish around to find sky coverage, often after dark, and downloading a channel list - also time-consuming.

At this writing, many RVers use Musk's Starlink. The initial equipment is expensive (although refurbished units are sometimes available). Starlink's hardware and data plans seem to change as often as the weather. But a larger issue is signal interference from trees, and, hey, what's a campground without trees. I'm told Starlink's newer dishes provide a wider capture angle, but interference is still a factor. Amazon is supposed to compete with Starlink soon. Perhaps competition will lower every RVer's costs.

Currently, I use T-Mobile's cellular gateway. Cellular service eliminates issues related to finding satellites for a dish, and so far the service has not capped my data – though on a busy Saturday night at a campground, a Netflix movie may buffer. T-Mobile's 5G gateway provides internet service inexpensively, and their newest gateway box has antenna ports. They "lend" it to you for free as long as you have service with them.

Before I got the new T-Mobile gateway, I spent hours pleading with them to give or sell one to me. Finally, after months and a couple of wrong equipment orders received, they sent me one. The new gateway coupled with a Waveform outside antenna provides the single most powerful improvement in reception that I've found – at a reasonable price.

To mount the antenna, I use a pole that extends in sections - like a flagpole - and I run it up the outside of my rig. A free smartphone app (Opensignal) lets me find the nearest cell tower to aim the antenna. But the antenna works well without aiming, so I often don't bother with that step.

So far, T-Mobile offers affordable internet, and unlike its rival carrier, I can actually reach T-Mobile tech support when I need to.

But there are rumors that T-Mobile intends to bump prices substantially on gateways used at locations that change. Word is that they will offer an AWAY plan at nearly triple the cost of some of their earlier monthly plans. Obviously, that would make a great product much less appealing to RVers.

(Up to now, although T-Mobile's official terms of service does limit the use of their gateway to the "home" location, it's a policy they haven't enforced. And T-Mobile reps have been promoting their internet gateway for use in RVs. But the best information at this writing is that T-Mobile's internet for changing locations is about to get pricey - bad news for RVers.)

Getting internet in the woods is one thing, but once you're online comes the question of how to get and stream the content you want.

The best streaming service I've found for RVers is YouTube TV. I use it with a Roku box and Roku remote because I find the Roku interface simple to use. But more important for RVers, I can use YouTube TV at home *and* where I camp.

I tried Hulu which has the shows I want and a nice interface, but Hulu make you register a new home location at every stop. They limit the number of times you can change your "home address." That doesn't work for RVers. YouTube TV occasionally asks me to verify that it is me when I arrive at a new location, but doing so is quick and simple.

If you don't know about Chris Dunphy and Cherie Ve Ard and the *Mobile Internet Resource Center (MIRC)* on YouTube and their website, they are everyone's pick for the best up-to-date resource on connectivity. RVers and boaters look to them to decipher plans and equipment from the better know providers. They do a great job of simplifying the complex and keeping us up to date in the world of internet services and hardware that changes at a blinding speed.

Now let me pause to put on my thick, black, professorial glasses and wax academic. The Oxford English Dictionary defines *glamping* as "a form of camping involving accommodation and facilities more luxurious than those associated with traditional camping."

As a devout couch potato, I have to wonder what drives me to regularly pay hundreds of dollars to stay at a campground so I can sit in my RV and stream the same TV news and watch the same Netflix movies that I see at home.

Hey, I never said I'm a model of rationality.

What a Waste

Okay so a trip to the dump station isn't on anyone's bucket list, and nobody has asked me over to watch slides of them dumping their black tank. But emptying my own black tank has provided me with opportunities to mess up.

Leaving campgrounds, I've forgotten to make sure my gray tank and black tank handles were in the closed position. So when I uncapped the sewer hose at our next stay, what splashed over me fell short of *eau de cologne*. I scurried to cap the hose and clean myself up as best I could.

I wised up and added a twist-on value gate. This inexpensive unit blocks the release of the excess sewage that collects at the cap. But since the valve gate twists on easily, unfortunately it twists off just as easily. I reenacted scenes from the Noah flood movie until I learned to add twist-on pressure to the gate with one hand while pulling the gate release handle with the other.

My 5th wheel has a black tank washout port that I use a lot. Sorry to be graphic, but my wife and I use an excessive amount of toilet paper, and though it's the quick-to-dissolve RV paper, I'm paranoid about it building up and coating the black tank.

Some folks pour ice in the back tank and go for a drive. Supposedly ice sloshing around cleans the tank. I haven't tried that, but besides adding treatment chemicals that tame order and facilitate paper breakdown, I repeatedly run water through the black tank's washout port until the water I see in my clear plastic hose adapter starts to look clear.

All of which provides me with another chance for a misadventure. While I wait for the blank tank washout port to fill, I'll tackle some small chore around the rig. Maybe I'll lubricate the slide out rubber or do a little polishing. Can you see where this is going? Once in a moment of high-level absentmindedness, I forgot that I was filling the black tank. Water started pouring out below the rig. Fortunately I as able to shut off the water before a pipe burst. I should wear a cowbell around my neck to remind me.

For me, those white drink-water-approved hoses turn rigid soon and get hard to pack. Instead, I use stainless steel water hoses that are flexible, kink free, and roll up easily after use. Since traveling RVers are constantly connecting hoses, I use quick connectors (male and female sets).

We try to steer clear of bottled water and travel with a Berkey filter canister. (The smaller Berkey canister is perfect for short term stays.) Water from the Berkey tastes good and the filters last years. The Berkey helps us minimize the use of bottled water which carries small plastic microbes in the water. It helps us reduce our contribution to the world supply of plastic bottle trash. Perhaps you've seen pictures of the Great Pacific Garbage Patch - an island of plastic bottles and waste in the ocean that's 620,000 square miles long - that's twice the size of the state of Texas.

We also attach a water filter to our hoses which helps limit how much sediment reaches our rig. If you've ever removed the anode tube to flush the hot water heater, you know how much sediment builds up from camp water.

The water pressure at campgrounds varies, so we protect our plumbing with a pressure regulator on the hose. We've tried using the simple brass regulator, but prefer one that includes an adjustable pressure gage. (That is if I can remember not to leave it in the rig over the winter so it still works in the spring. Yes, I've screwed that up too.)

Rodents, Rats and RVs

On several occasions I've been fired up and ready to leave for the great outdoors — or in my case, in the great RV indoors with TV — but our departure stalled. *Rats!*

That's the cause of the delay, not a curse. Rats and mice, feeling unwelcome, have taken matters into their own teeth to mess up our travel plans.

Several times the delay has been a turn signal or brake light that didn't work, and driving a long rig without working turn signals is asking for trouble. Twice rats come to dine have ordered the specialty of the house - our cooper wire entrée with a delicious topping of red plastic. I wish the problem was an easy fix like a bulb replacement. Instead, the coach's underbelly covering had to be removed and a new wire run.

Rodent "rash" is common for RVers. I'm told it's worse some years than others. I've tried every Mickey Mouse suggestion anyone's offered: traps, poison, Irish Spring soap, and an electric sonic wave machine. I've placed bags of pleasant-smelling peppermint throughout the rig and bait traps. I've done my best to spray foam over underbelly openings, and put steel wool in gaps.

My conclusion? In the end, I wave a white flag when I see a rodent. They win, I lose. The pros tell me they haven't yet found a perfect solution. So after all is said and done, I end up asking my dealer to get the taillight or turn signal working again so we can leave.

Sometimes the better part of valor is to know when a superior enemy has beaten you.

A Doctor in the House?

One morning Susan came to me, "We've got to take a vacation and soon."

"What's the rush?" I said.

"Because we can still fit all your meds into a steamer trunk," she quipped.

Which brings me to the subject of pills, health, and locating a doctor when you travel. Luckily, we haven't had significant medical issues while RVing, but thank goodness for Medicare and drop in medical facilities. I recall two small medical issues.

Susan wears earrings for pierced ears, and now and then she'll take them out to give her ear a rest. But once she didn't for a long period, and the small jewel began to work its way in and embed in her ear. She's not a complainer, but I saw her wincing.

Our GPS located a drop-in medical service on our route. The doctor did a bit of light surgery and got the earring out. Susan's discomfort ended, and her ear was fine in a few days. Rather than wait hours in a hospital emergency room, we prefer visiting drop-in medical facilities for minor issues.

For reasons I won't bore you with, I try to wear contacts lenses for better vision. I'm the worst contact lens inserter ever to get loose from a ophthalmologist's office. I love my lenses and see really well with them. But I struggle endlessly to get them in or out. A high percentage of the time, they end up in the sink, or lost somewhere in the bathroom – almost anywhere except in my eyes. (The floor of our RV has 20-20 vision. I thought of hosting a scavenger hunt for the campground.)

I also rip my contact lenses regularly. On one RV trip, I ripped a lens trying to remove it, but I could only find a portion of it. I figured the missing fragment must have fallen somewhere and forgot about it.

A day later, looking like Rudolph the Red Eye Reindeer, I visited a drop-in medical service. They couldn't find the fragment and sent me to a hospital that had an ophthalmologist. The excellent doctor had a powerful magnifying instrument and located the tiny culprit. He removed it, and in a day one could see again what the commander at the Battle of Bunker Hill called the "whites" of my eye.

I haven't opted for one of the RV travel insurance upgrades that reimburse for hotel expenses or provide help to get your RV back home in the event of an incapacitating illness - though I see the value of such a plan.

Me and My RV

BY NOW, YOU'VE CONCLUDED TWO things about me and my misadventures on the metaphoric wrong side of the road.

First, that I'm not a guy you want along on your next trip. I could curse your holiday.

Second, you may wonder with all my misadventures, and the thousands I've spent attributable to low brain wattage, why in the world am I still RVing? Is it worth it?

My answer is a resounding *yes*.

In my post-corporate life, three subjects have always fascinated me because there is so much more to learn. First, computers continue to challenge me. Does anyone ever feel they know all there is to know about the hardware, the software or the operating system?

I felt that way as a pilot as I worked my way to each higher license. Changing aviation technology and changing rules of the air meant that keeping up required determination.

Finally, I continue to be drawn to and keep learning more about RVing. There's always an exciting new rig like the Pebble to ogle. Or I'll learn of a repair trick or hear about a new accessory that makes camping easier, safer, or more fun.

I learn more about my hobby – if that's what RVing is - with each trip I take and every YouTube video I watch. My blunders have been lessons that taught me what not to do.

So when the hunger for a change of scenery takes hold again, my RV will take me to new vistas, new dining experiences and often to meet new friends. Why would I ever want to give that up?

And, as with my days of working in the cruise industry, I travel without having to schlep from hotel to hotel or to pack, unpack and repack at each stop.

RVing means I get to travel with my wife and our two four-legged backseat drivers. (Does that total three backseat drivers?)

I get pained if I even have to think about waving goodbye to my pups who look at me longingly, panting, wondering where their dad's going, and why I'm not leashing them up to take them along. Since I can't explain to them that I'll be back soon, my RV means the issue doesn't have to come up at all.

It's great too that more and more American restaurants are following the European tradition of welcoming well-behaved dogs that come to dine with their occasionally well-behaved masters.

Finally and importantly, every time I climb the foldout steps and enter my little, safe, rolling cocoon, a spell falls over me. We all live in a pressure cooker world, and if we have a place to escape tension, shouldn't we cherish it? My RV provides a sense of peace I don't find anywhere else.

I may be growing a bit "long in the tooth," but I'll be RVing as long as I can hook up my rig and head safely down a highway to some new and exotic locale.

What's not to like? What's not to love?

OTHER BOOKS BY I. MICHAEL GROSSMAN

Non-Fiction

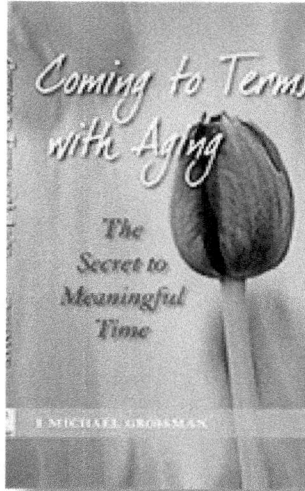

Coming to Terms with Aging: the Secret to Meaningful Time, RDR books

Memoir

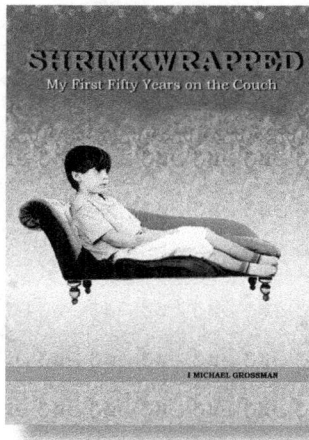

Shrinkwrapped: my first fifty years on the couch, RDR Books

An Adult Children's Adventure

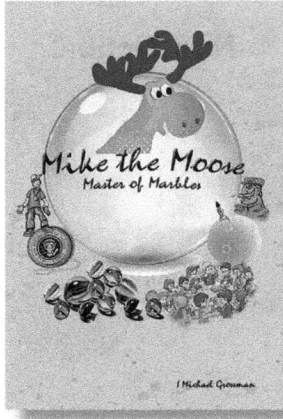

Mike the Moose: Master of Marbles, EBook Bakery

Fiction

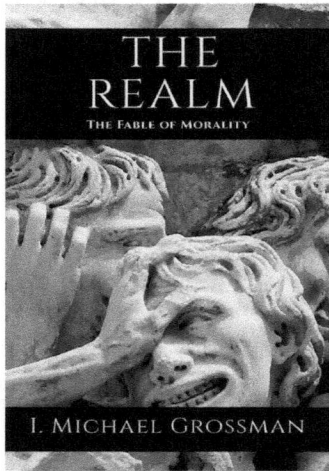

The Realm - the Fable of Morality - EBook Bakery

Poetry

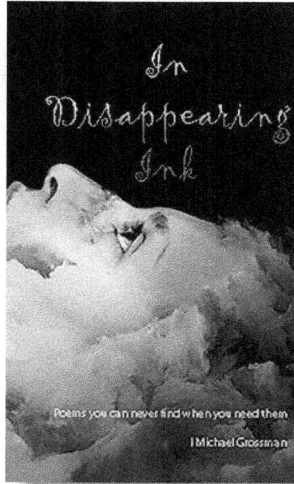

In Disappearing Ink: poems you can never find when you need them - EBook Bakery

Political Satire/Science Fiction

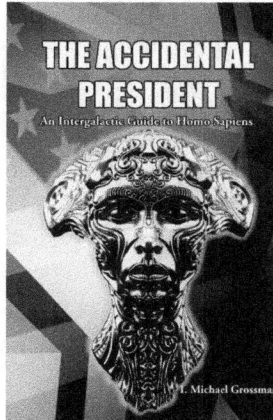

The Accidental President,
An Intergalactic Guide to Homo Sapiens - EBook Bakery

Fiction/Personal Evolution

The Power
What would you do with the power to be invisible?
- EBook Bakery

Poetry

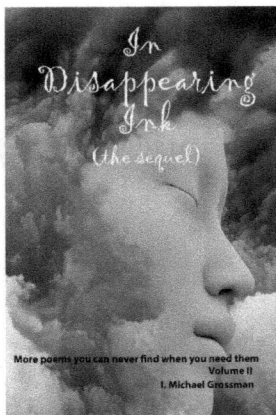

In Disappearing Ink: Part two of poems you can never find when you need them - EBook Bakery

60

ABOUT THE AUTHOR

RVing on the Wrong Side of the Road, is I. Michael Grossman's ninth book. His genres run the gamut from fiction, non-fiction, and poetry to what he calls his "adult children's book".

His articles span similarly diverse topics including those published in *Advertising Age, Ergo Solutions* magazine, *The CLIA Cruise Industry Annual Report, The American Banker,* and *Plane & Pilot* magazine.

Grossman holds a B.A. and M.A. from Michigan State University, and he taught English and Journalism at Oakland Community College. While the VP of Marketing for Norwegian American Cruises and Salen Lindblad Cruises, he created *The Science of Your Own Success,* a course taught at the New School in New York before he started four businesses including Cruises of Distinction and Office Organix.

"I sold my last business because I had a book to write," says Grossman, referring to his memoir, *Shrinkwrapped: my first fifty years on the couch.*

Grossman, whose books have been traditionally published and self-published, currently runs the EBookBakery.com which helps other authors publish.

"The 'I.' in my name is not an abbreviation. The full name on my birth certificate actually is I. Michael Grossman. I claim no responsibility for the name, although I participated at the birth," quips Grossman.

Please help by offering your review at Amazon,
B&N or others booksellers. Thank you!

www.ingramcontent.com/pod-product-compliance
Lightning Source LLC
Chambersburg PA
CBHW060426050426
42449CB00009B/2148